POSTMORTEM

To Marianne,
Before CSI,
there was:

POSTMORTEM

POEMS BY

Maurice Kilwein Guevara

Maurice Kilwein Guevara

31 Jan. 2005
Marshall, MN

The University of Georgia Press

ATHENS AND LONDON

© 1994 by Maurice Kilwein Guevara
All rights reserved
Published by the University of Georgia Press
Athens, Georgia 30602

Designed by Betty Palmer McDaniel
Set in 10/13 Galliard
by Tseng Information Systems, Inc.
Printed and bound by Thomson-Shore, Inc.
The paper in this book meets the guidelines for
permanence and durability of the Committee on
Production Guidelines for Book Longevity of the
Council on Library Resources.

Printed in the United States of America

98 97 96 95 94   C   5   4   3   2   1
98 97   P   5   4   3   2

Library of Congress Cataloging in Publication Data
Kilwein Guevara, Maurice.
Postmortem : poems / by Maurice Kilwein Guevara.
       p.   cm.
ISBN 0-8203-1561-3 (alk. paper)
—ISBN 0-8203-1562-1 (pbk.: alk. paper)
I. Title.
PS3557.I4135P67   1994
811'.54—dc20   93-12346

British Library Cataloging in Publication Data available

We're all immigrants to this reality.
Victor Hernández Cruz

Acknowledgments

The author and publisher gratefully acknowledge the following publications in which these poems first appeared:

Cream City Review: "Postmortem"
Exquisite Corpse: "Plum-Dark Humor," "The Young Beast Devours Kafka" (as "Self-Portrait, By Kafka")
New Growth Arts Review: "Absence," "The Explanation," "Tepteptep"
Parnassus: Poetry in Review: "Tuesday Shaman"
Pendulum: "Angela Wandering"
Poetry: "Cofradía," "Tombstones"
Shepherd Express: "The Buddy Holly Poem"
Wisconsin Academy Review: "The Long Woman Bathing" (as "The Man in the Room"), "Our Marriage"

Contents

Foreword

POSTSCRIPT

Postmortem

Even the corpse has its own beauty.
Emerson

These lips of Mr. Tunis Flood are cornflower
Blue. I have a set of cups like that.
I bring my ear to his heart but hear no murmur,
No vibrato, no baroque flutter of blood.
I love Pathology because there's never any rush.
I sip my coffee. Think. Write, "Nipples the color of avocados."
(How beautiful they are in the fluorescent light.)

Time to open and discover now the exquisite
Essence of Tunis Flood. Syringe: prick—
Vitreous humor for the fellows in the lab.
On my little radio Scarlatti plays, and when my door
Hinge creaks, it speaks. "Hello," it says. I

Concentrate. Write, "Tardieu's spots
Bruise the livid skin. Like violets in a shade."
With my favorite knife I trace a line from heart
To chin. From sternum to pubis. I watch a man bloom,
And remove, remove. Each organ I weigh and record.
Perhaps I should have been a postman
To send my friends and lovers away,

Boxed, in parts. Why is there wind
In this windowless room? Where is my mallet,
My chisel? There: crack.
The calvarium slides out
Like a baby, I hold your brain,
Mr. Flood, and wonder what matter
Holds back the rush of memories.
And in what soft ridge lies the vision of your death?

AMERICA
I

Mountainsong

Bacatá: the world greens
on the mountainwalk down
take your time
take three thousand days
one for each orchid you find
the air warms
as you listen to the birds
the yellow blur humming
treesongs   macaw
parrot   parrot
heron   there in the water
to learn family
speak two hundred tongues
to sing human history
walk backwards for seven thousand years
by the river where bats swarm at twilight
remember the blood
and the blood will be alive

Violentólogo

You discover the moment of that first Spanish sword
coming down out of the blue coastal sky
hacking a fatal wound deep between two ribs
the native man backfalling
no magic then from the open bloody mouth
at the side of the body
no green spirit stalk or sudden flowering
from that hole ripped wider
by the beaks of feeding birds
the thorough armies of tiny red ants
and windy time until the bleached skeleton
lay covered completely in white sand

Tuesday Shaman

Say it is Tuesday
that he sits beside the road,
slowly chewing a shaft of snapdragons,
the red liquid rolling down his throat.
He flicks his magic tongue to read the air:
one is falling in love,
one is coming to him with a question,
one is dreaming of warm bread,
one is combing her mother's hair in the city
when a stray bullet enters her soft skull
(then the dark child sleeps forever)—
everything he tastes is written on the wind.

I have thought about it.
Now I'm not sure.
It may be some other day (not Tuesday)
that he sings death in three languages,
in the English language,
in the Spanish language,
in the Chibcha tongue of dreams,
belching a perfumed breath,
volcanoes in his palm,
counting the infinities,
rolling cut cornflowers through his hair,
mourning once again the four crazy loves
that left him sitting beside the road.

Campesino, 1948

Have you ever found your brother?

Last year the police brought me an arm
they said was his, same fingerprints.
It was blackened from the jungle,
a railroad spike right through his wrist—
they also gave me a piece of paper.

What did the paper say?

I can't read, but they said it closes the case.
They listed his death as an accident.

What did you do with the arm of your brother?

I called for a priest, but he refused to come.
He said an arm wasn't worth the bother
of a last sacrament.

What then did you do with the arm?

I keep it in a glass box
with fresh flowers
by the window.
I pray and talk to him.

The glass keeps the bees away.

Fear

The tight syllable Angela had swallowed in late fall
by May

had sprouted forth from her mouth a long,
dark-branching sentence:

pink and white blossoms, green buds,
wet bark beneath the blue, death at every node.

Cofradía

How many times do I have to tell you Yes
I wear the black hood of a common saint
following stars and the smell of *basuco*
straight in my mission as the one bullet
cutting a way through the fifteen years
of your crazy skull   The moon
empties of her marrow in the dirt
I lay on you a dark rose whose stem
cannot hold the petals   Dead One
I walk away
leaving the three spirits
to do their work in peace
as I will do mine
Tomorrow is another night   O missionaries
we are brothers on the dark road

How many times do I have to tell you

Violence

Instead of a cosmos of violets
stuffed in the mouth
of an eight-year-old *muchachito*
lying face-up on his bed
his small
perfect
testicles

Tombstones

An Angel stands, she and her black wings invisible
to the young man working in the Andes sun—

There is a truck packed full with headstones
stolen in moonlight. The young entrepreneur
works alone with shovel and dream; someday
he will be as famous as Andrew Carnegie or
Buddha.

His heart is a bird of fire,
and the Colombian sun is hot as he rises
to remove another tombstone and drag it
to the workplace where his tools are.
North south east west: four German Shepherds
surround him; he is the center of his star.

Then the awful racket as the electric grinder
starts up, and down on stone the abrasion begins
to erase the names of the dead: Edgar Antonio Botero
                              Evaristo Llanos
                              Jaime Betancourt
                              Isabel Pinilla

Antonio Cante
Féliz Lozado
Jorge Millán
Dora Cifuentes . . . making room for the future—

And the Angel flies off like any prophet,
her shadow moving slowly north, over the countryside.

The Birth of the Young Beast

Once upon a rhyme hatched faraway and high
in the green mountains of Colombia
came the little laughing *bestia*.
(There is a will to fly.)
Out of stardust,
out of spiritsyllable,
out of *semilla* and sunrays,
out of the obsidian shell
of all his nulled minutes,
he kicked his way with chromium hooves
(the size and shine of coffee spoons)
and tucked his batwings close.
¿Qué me cuentas? his first words, friendly.
How strange the crowding humans were,
crossing themselves or dropping
(plop plop on the wooden floor)
like flies.

Abuelo, Answers and Questions

1

Abuelo, why are there flies?
They're reporters for the dead, mi joven bestia.
What do they report?
If the millonarios *won or lost.*

2

Abuelo?
What?
I forgot.

3

Abuelo, who puts the scorpion in my bed when I'm asleep?
Why, is there one when you wake?
Yes.
Dead?
Yes.
Don't worry. The dead don't sting.

4

Abuelo?
What?
How old am I?
Almost five years old.

How old are you?
Old as bones. When the moon was born,
I was already eight years old. . . .
When I was a boy, I lived on the coast of Colombia
and rode the fins of blue whales at night
from Barranquilla to Nantucket Island
and back, this before dawn.

5

Abuelo, why do I have steel hooves?
To kick truth in the ass.
Abuelo, why do I have shiny hooves?
To dance a little cumbia. To play with mirrors.
Abuelo, why do I have hooves?
Because they run in the family.

Abuelo, Abuelo

"   "
the *abuelo* answered
because he was dead.
Every gourd shook with grief,
mourning. It was the dry season.

It was the windy time of Colombia:
crazed bones
exposed
out of the cracked earth
knocked and clicked
to the rhythm of a cumbia
played in the bright air.

A random Tuesday of the year
the little boy
(el joven bestia)
alone
found his grandfather
stonestill in the front room.

Abuelo's eyes: wide
dead and filled with sunlight.
Across one globe a greenbottle
fly making a pilgrimage
stopped
to rub its front
legs together.
Like sticks for fire.
A quick prayer.
Then the cold business

of laying eggs
in moisture
perfectly . . .
and of moving on
like one more saint
crossing the arc of paradise.

The Magic Carpet

What you need to know
happened two weeks before
the little creature
(with three teeth missing)
found his grandfather
splayed out on an Oriental rug.
The rug was a gift from long ago,
the family's only possession.

A fortnight earlier
a national burial tax
went into effect,
legislated from the mountainous
and faraway capital of Bogotá.
The tax was the brainchild
of a young senator from Tunja:
So many *pesos* per corpse,
per interment,
would be extracted
like golden teeth
from each grieving family.

But the little creature,
his mother and his father
could not afford the indignity
of the new tax. So
that Wednesday morning
before breakfast
they wrapped the *abuelo*
in the Oriental rug,
and the father carefully

loaded the grandfather
and a shovel
onto the bed of the old truck.
The plan was to drive
deep into the hills
and make a private ceremony.

But the little boy grew hungry.
And the father grew hungry.
And the mother needed food also.
So they stopped somewhere
for twenty minutes
to eat. When they returned,
the mother began to cry:
¿Dónde está? ¿Dónde está Papá?
The Oriental rug was gone and instantly
the father prayed to San Cristóbal
as the mute child studied the shovel
pointing east.

Gold Dust

¡Ay qué trabajo me cuesta
quererte como te quiero!
                    Lorca

1

I have no heart to sing.
There is only this bird
(hooded starling)
caged in me
hesitant beneath the cluster
of dark berries.

2

It is always fall.
The wind is forever alive
where I find myself
thirty beneath the twisting tree
in the shadow of yellow leaves.

3

I unbar me:
hew the bones and years,
watch the gold dust fall,
reach in,
hold her with my hands,
saying over her:

I have no heart to sing
then let go
to be the blue
turning silence.

Angela Manrique

(grenade victim, Colombia, 1963)

If I say the moon,
will you know what I mean?
And if I cut cloth to hear the tearing,
if I'm not hungry,
if I study only the relief of your hands,
if I talk of clotted hair,
if I stare at your dress hanging on a nail,
if I dream three nights of the shattered bell
then wake and walk out into the yard
to wash my face and hands,
swirling the moon down the rain bucket,
and if I say nothing to you at all . . .

Know I was last to hold the body of Angela Manrique.

Angela Errante

En Abril el serio azul
de la tarde avanzada
        luego de aclarar
un frío
        la larga, demacrada sombra de un niño
            corriendo
música flúida como Mozart
        hubiera hecho una mañana
                    (nota
            las húmedas campanillas
            deprimidas por una sola
            pisada)
Fluyen impresiones de Monet,
descendiendo
                una hueca rasgadura de la tierra
        encuentro flores silvestres:
                lirios anaranjados o amarillos
tantas amapolas
            rojas y erguidas como llamas
y brotando de mi muslo un retoño
                        de flor azul
        Me levanto soñolienta
ahuyentando vagas sensaciones de vértigo
me acerco al huerto de manzanos lisiados
            cada uno calavera arraigada
repleto de capullos—
                    profusiones de flores
            (racimos de pensamientos y milagros)
sopla
        blanco-polilla en el adormecido viento,
                        anochecer

opacando el olor
        de la luz
                llego a los
planos campos arados
            matiz de ceniza
y me postro en el suave
               pálido polvo
       Del pueblo
campana alguna toca la melodía de las nueve
      (¿y adónde se han ido los pájaros amarillos?)

Angela Wandering

In April the serious blue
of late afternoon
        after the clearing
a chill
        long, gaunt shadow of a child
                running
a music fluid as Mozart
        made any morning
                        (note
        the watered trilliums
        depressed by a single
        footfall)
Flow of Monet's impressions,
descending
                a hollow, rend in the earth,
        I find wildflowers:
                        irises orange or yellow
so many poppies
                red and straight as flares
and bursting from my thigh a shoot
                of cornflower blue
                I rise sleepy
shake off weak signals of vertigo
approach the orchard of crippled apple trees
                each rooted skull
heavier with bloom—
                profusions of flowers
        (thought clusters and miracles)
blow
        moth-white in the drowsy wind,
                evening

obscuring the scent
       of light
          I arrive at
flat plowed fields
       the shade of ashes
and kneel in the soft
       pale dust
     From town
no bells ringing the melody of nine
        (and where have the yellow birds gone?)

AMERICA
II

The Bridge

His first surprise in this new America is unspoken:
Snow. It floats down out of the gray white up,
falling, touching his wings like puffs of chalk:
No more. More now. Falling cold slowly all
around him, like a million stars. He looks up
at his mother, who is changed.

                She is older in the snowlight,
smiling. *Nieve.* But her word comes only as a steam puff.
Language falling away, in the world becoming white.
The little beast is five years old. Everything
begins to shake and roar. Snow and beneath
his feet the world begins again. *Ferrocarril,*
she shouts out, like a horn or bell he cannot hear.

Burning Hill

This is a love poem to Diego de Landa,
this is a lullaby, sleepwalker, from me to you:

Listen to the chain burning through pine rings,
blowing gold dust in a flurry down the spikes of sun.

The sounds you hear—the hundreth groan and crack,
the coming down of trees—leave you silent.

When the trucks ascend with their enormous wheels
to carry away the logs stacked like pyramids

to lumberyards, paper mills, furnaces of paradise,
take wine with me, and corn bread on this new stone.

Watch the men raze the brush with fire to clear the field,
ignite a heap of branches in the growing dark. Yawn and pray:

This is four hundred years and far away in Pennsylvania.
By morning on the scarred hill there are no birds, deer,

only the seed child throwing grass to right and left
under a blue sky. The cemetery is open at last;

the first grave is dug. Wake, Diego de Landa,
we're needed to lift and carry. Kiss me before we start.

John Kane

This is a true story about the immigrant Kane,
how a hundred years ago in Pittsburgh he painted boxcars
black in the filthy car yards of the Baltimore & Ohio,
one after another until lunchtime. On his break
he'd mix up brighter colors; one side of the next
boxcar would be his wide, steel canvas. In the plain style,
high as he could reach with the green brush,
he'd make hills grow up, dreaming always of Scotland.
Up a stepladder he'd climb to have the sky
a field of pure blue and clouds
floating away, above the highland.
Down on earth he'd put two small girls beside a river,
a red maple, and the words *John Kane*
just as the whistle blew.

At one o'clock he'd start to cover his work with black paint.

The Old Worker

*I never reached the point where I failed
to see beauty that is everywhere about.*
J.K.

Eyes closed, mouth on the tin whistle
Blowing out the tune of *Drowsy Maggie,*
John Kane knew the secret to angel-making
Was as simple as finding a child. I picture

Some eight-year-old in Pittsburgh crawling out
Of wooden cellar doors at dawn. On the small
Blades of his back I draw wings.
I paint his plummage fine and white,

Waiting till he rises,
And bounces the light air,
Tumbling soft space
      above red bricks and the cinder tiles,
      above even the orange blast firing the Mon.

34

Revelation 3,000

Summer starts at home and stretches two chalk lines
running forever   O, Clemente   at night the boy dreams
backpedaling to the warning track   to the fence
at the edge of the world and beyond   weightless
outfielder of the universe   tumbling and chasing
in his eighth light year with the Time Pirates
down down a falling star   he is alone

caught in a rundown between the blue earth and the bone-
bright desert of the moon   O, Clemente
which way should he lean
what should he do with his island eyes to deceive the second
baseman   how pump his arms to suggest pure speed
slowing down to freeze the pose forever like a photograph
then *go*   best to slide into that ocean roar headfirst
like a diver   like a dolphin   like the hungriest gull

rhythm   rhythm is the thing that swings through time
the boy steps out of the batter's box   considers the wind
notes the precision of the stars ceiling the coliseum   re-
enters and broods   crosses himself for power
O, Clemente   the boy breathes and concentrates
on the dime of light fired from the mound
now he swings   now he knows that a single is
the connection of desire and act   the solitary kiss of waking

the Young Beast tells his mother that someday he will fly
(she thinks he's still dreaming) to help the merciful, Black Saint.

Plum-Dark Humor

David teaches history to children. Today
he is showing them a film of the war
in Vietnam. "America," he explains,
"was defending the South," as he watches
what he'd seen as a child from the living room floor.
Some of the children have decided to put their heads
down. And David doesn't feel well
sitting in the small chair.

Two images are clearest in his mind:
the naked girl on fire, running,
and this man, hands bound behind him,
being pushed, a small crowd nearby.
Another person, khaki uniform, holding a gun,
enters into view, waves the people back with his pistol,
fires into the man's brain and, bent,
the man falls sideways. Blood pumps and flows
warmly from his temple, oozes, slows,
forming a puddle on the dried-mud road.
David feels dizzy, tries to turn the projector off,
but instead switches the control to REVERSE.

And the dead man's mind draws
the blood back in, and the corpse flies up,
straightening out, and stands as instantly
the wound heals; the murderer waves the crowd on,
walking backwards out of the picture.

Some of the children are laughing.

Down

So he's thirteen
and the caseworker says What?
and the kid goes I wasted the motherfucker
and the caseworker says Well how come?
and the kid starts picking at his ear
and the kid keeps picking at his ear
Well how come?
and the kid says To bring him down
and keeps picking at the hole where his earring goes
and the caseworker gets kind
dead eyes and asks What for?
What else? How come?
and the kid turns back
and starts talking to nothing
like he's talking to the light bulb
saying Cause there he was all in the blood
Cause he was down
Cause he was down

He made the motherfucker down

The Young Beast at the Wreck

The voice brings him out of his first apartment
to the night street. Not the great steel shearing
crash, the perpendicular collision of Nova
under eighteen-wheeler, at the nexus of this street
and that. But the voice of the truck driver screaming
all his pain under the city stars.

Men from a corner
bar stand beside the shining wreckage,
listen to the hiss of the engine,
and one by one they speak:
Looks like a girl.
Ran a red light.
The steering column right through her.
Kid, kid, hey, get that guy off the street.

He watches himself drag
the butchered voice that is the universe
to the sidewalk.

The Young Beast Devours Kafka

Father, remember the hut where I changed to swim?
Remember my terror of the cold water?
I was six years old, a sickly specimen,
and you were the Giant who held my hand.

Now strange and thin,
your roots press and break
down through chest and skull. Here,
your gray wounded bark. And the branches,
their wind-strained power of iron, large,
the March oak of love and fear.

Love of fear you taught
in the mud-weight of your boots.

And so I have spent my obscure moods
hiding in the grotesque wood of imagination
where a white spider swings on his string
deadly and mushrooms puff spores,
where insane winds chant my Kaddish
and black, fur-soft mammals
falling through the long night
cut me to draw blood.

Because you said it was my work
to cut a way within myself
for crisis and failure,
Father, I should thank you.

Walking Home Alone, After a Reading,
the Young Beast Mocks a Star

Nothing is too small for my sarcasm.
G.S.

O, Carnegie-Mussolini University!

I, lucky Gerald, am wandering along the Iowa River,
or the Monongahela to the splendid Ohio.
My ears are white wings folded back,
and my left hand is feathered with a check
for three thousand dollars:
I have been reading again!
I am walking down Fifth Avenue in Oakland
and stop at the Mellon Bank
where all the tellers think I'm Allen Ginsberg.
I slowly deposit my dry seeds. Nothing comes
easy. I waited forty years for the fame.
Now it fits like a dark suit I've fattened into,
something I might wear at my own funeral,
as I stand before the black coffin filled with new poems.
Today I sang to the rich children about Blake
and how he saved my life three summers running.
About Jack and how true we were in the Paris of 1950.
And now how easily the lightest rain or snowfall
melting on my face can smear the blue cosmetics.
Today I alternated between melancholy and anger,
between the staged moan and the wild chant. A mad rabbi,
I sang against Henry Clay Frick.
I sang against the barges shipping death to Homestead.
I prayed for the angels in the middle of the earth,
flying with black lung. I painted the Mon Valley rusting away

and sang against money and power.
In Hebrew I shouted at God and death.
In the end I could not hear my singing
for the clapping was like an avalanche of fired coal.

The Workshop Deconstructs
the Young Beast

Kleist's Letter to Gabriela

Dear Gabriela,

    Argentina,
    Esta campana inútil.
    Ararat of faith.
    Harmonica.
    Harpsichord—
    Austria.
    A Dwarf hops.
    To Belgium:
    Matins and bells.
    Belencito,
    Colombia . . .
    Esta voz muerta de mi madre.
    El nueve de Abril:
    Cuba.
    Cyprus.
    I was so happy to see you.
    In Czechoslovakia?
    In a coffin?
    In Denmark,
    Pouring green tea.
    England and
    Half-tones of flugelhorns.
    Chrysalis. Estonia.
    My heart filling with rainwater.
    Finland and

Tinkling cowbells.
Fibers of a distaff.
Francis, the Saint.
Germany,
Vast cemetery of my youth.

In the creative writing class, located in a room on the fifth floor of the Cathedral of Learning, "I have a problem," Maurice said, grinning at his reflection in a teaspoon, "with the beginning of this poem."

Janet, the instructor, interrupted: "My question is, is it really a poem?"

"It's epistolary," Heather noted, pointing to the title.

"Yes," we all said in unison. "It's certainly not a sonnet."

"But it is poetic," Joe offered.

"But it's not narrative," Maurice added.

Melancholy, the Dwarf labeled it a non-narrative-multicultural-post-something poem.

"It's single-spaced," Michael observed. "I thought we weren't supposed to single-space."

"Is that really cogent?" the Young Beast wondered, looking over to Janet.

Janet touched her lips. The signal was clear: he should refrain from comment and allow the other twelve students to contribute their ideas.

"Well, Granger?" she asked.

"He writes weirdly."

I raised my hand.

"Yes?" Janet asked.

"I think the reason that the writer single-spaced was to make us aware of vertical dwellings. No?"

The Young Beast shook his head several times from east to west.

The Dwarf moaned, "Why do you have me hopping? I think it's cruel. I'm a human being, you know, and I have a soul just like anyone else." He began to cry into the rabbit-fur of his beard.

43

"You know what I just realized: This is a list," Kate said.

It clicked. Roberta mumbled, "Like the German composer, Franz Liszt."

"Hungarian," Monroe said in clarification.

Maurice responded, "That's it." He put his teaspoon down. "It stops at Germany. Don't you see? Hungary would have been next."

The Dwarf could stand it no longer. He was bawling quite hysterically, so much that his chest hair had become matted. Maurice was now staring at his own reflection in the window that was not open. One of the white fluorescent tubes of light blinked off.

"Shall we take a break?" Janet suggested, whereupon the Dwarf hopped out of his seat and through the open window. Such a long, sick, human squeak he made, as he fell the three blurred stories to his death.

> Greece,
> Yannis:
> "Clearly he went out of his way
> to avoid saying the word d e a t h."
> Then Hungary,
> Bells ringing the melody of nine—
> My long spells of silence.
> Schizophrenic Ireland:
> Father and of the Son and of the Holy Ghost.
> Israel,
> There is fresh blood on the wall.
> Italia,
> "La figlia che piange."
> "Who I am," the Dwarf wonders,
> As he plucks the soft petals of stars.
> And Jamaica . . .
> "An de rydim a de Rhumbo,
> An de rydim a de Shango."
> Latvia with
> Triangles ringing . . .

Of Lebanon
All I remember is the soldier—
A dead infant in his raised fist.
Lithuania.

Everyone sat around the rectangular table, some with cans of Tab, some with Mr. Pibb, each with the sick feeling that he should have done something for the Dwarf. Made from Spirit Masters, their papers were stapled and bluish, with the thumb print of the Young Beast on page four. The typescripts offered no peace of mind. A voice through a loudspeaker was heard ordering the students to clear away from the suicide.

I took out my rabbit's foot and rubbed it.

Maurine smiled reassuringly.

We tried to comfort each other in our grief. In homage to the Dwarf, we all said how much we admired his sensitivity to line breaks.

Netherlands,
A field of strawberries at night.
Norway,
Faraway and northern.
Perú—Uru-
Bamba of watermusic.
Poland's
Cold soft ashes of the dead.
Portugal:
Slowly watering flowers of laughter.
Russia. Fireflies
Blink.
South Africa burning,
"But I am a man addicted to hope."
Sri Lanka,
Bombs in the lunchboxes of children.
And Sweden,
We think it's like winter, like Eden.

Their collective grief was being transformed into anger, and so they turned to the Young Beast. "You're the one who should deal with this guilt you are making us feel. And we're tired of waiting for this alleged letter of yours. We don't think there is a letter. We think you're a big fucking fraud," said the stone-faced peers.

The Young Beast just sat, touching his beard. Tomorrow he would be twenty. He heard sirens coming up Forbes Avenue.

> Switzerland:
> The Dwarf was listening.
> Taiwan
> Is like hearing through fog.
> Thailand.
> I will be an island: Gorgona.

Then Janet asked, "If you would . . . why would you write this letter?"

It was a reflex. "Because I love you all," he said. And the words came:

Like the fibers of a distaff, everything is tangled in my mind; ambition is taut with annihilation. Think of some mechanical arm built of red wires and blue arteries, holding in its metal fingers, depending upon perspective, either a soft quill or a silver knife. What makes a mood so precarious that, if good, it crudely dissipates like morning fog? Tell me what mixture of sleep and thought precipitates my long spells of silence, star and moonlight moving through leaves of the hanging plants. I am the pale animal of the dark room.

You would discover me inside of you, a tiny beast with many tongues, a conceptus, still.

Here, listen: the left auricle of my heart is filling with rainwater, and the apple trees near the stable are wet and flowering, and the wind is continuous through the spine of the hearth. A spring storm will pass, you would tell me. But why, must everything blow away?

In music there is horror, in sickness a timeless beauty, like two nerve patterns of lightning, white veins, jagging across the human eye. Lift and shake out a roll of sheet metal—to mock thunder.

Now, a peasant girl slaughters a sow pinned between her legs. Her fingers and arms are brown and bloodstained. Fireflies blink.

Soon the sun will rise.

Gabriela, please don't write to me again. My only wish is to die.

Yours,
K.

Our Marriage

One afternoon in Athens
I saw a beggar squatting
on a dry road, an arm outstretched
and hand opened: Around him so many
silver drachmae were thrown, each glittering.
He'd been dead since the clanging of noon bells.

The Young Beast in Spring

Thoreau. *The whistle of the locomotive penetrates*
memory. That was the spring of my new boots,

walking the tracks of the B&O, fallen ladders,
boxcars, coffins, stolen dream songs. To survive

your twentieth year in Pittsburgh, Pennsylvania,
you must learn to fly above the rivers, and suffer

the mills to rust away. And forever bury the dead
in those hills and in your sleep. There's always work.

That April I mounted the steps of the Carnegie Library,
clacking like a goat. Hooved dreamer of the dark stacks,

don't be deceived. You may never reach the sky hooks.
If you find that book by the painter Kane, mind first

the picture of the murdered Christ, not the sweet words:
I never reached the point where I failed to see beauty

that is everywhere about. By then he was an old man
with one leg, a tin whistle, and green time. Walden.

Thoreau, Berryman, Kane, Gilbert, *known liars all:*
In spring I proved my voice, in the throat of a tunnel.

The Long Woman Bathing

Although he can not admit it even to himself,
these are the years whose possibility he has always dreaded.

The man in the room listens to cars and rain, unfolds
maps that have failed him, lines tracing absence along the dark
    interstate.

If a friend were to call him on the telephone,
the man would drawl, "It's like I'm being stalked in a dream."

In the gray light of the television it happens that he awakens
on the floor and studies his overcoat hanging, remembering the
    old self.

He is twenty again and running in the museum from room to
    white room
where he finds her in the Bonnard, the long woman bathing in
    the lilac water.

And were it possible at any moment he might cry out:
I refuse her ghost, I refuse to dart like a deer in the open.

Eye of the Buck

Hind hooves
    tied
   hanging from
    a porch,
the solitary buck.

2

Tonight it will rain.

3

The brown animal suggests the land:
the gut
        of woods and hills,
ribs like railroad ties
        like fallen ladders leading to nowhere—
antlers
    the tangle of branches—

4

The buck sways, hangs in the wind.

5

By morning the sky
will be blue. Everything you see
will be frozen.

6

Arc of the eye, brown as beer glass.

The Young Beast Mourns
a Right Turn

Down Liberty Avenue this Thursday, July 4, 1991,
the delicious reminiscence of his and whore
sweat figging him pungent. Love's a war.
The Young Beast marches in a parade of one,
self-cast in the moral drama: Everyman, Adam,
the American, Batman, Young Goodman Brown.
Ribbons pink or yellow ringing each
bloody digit: Noon bells and explosions!
Fist in the air, watch him wave his flag—
a gargantuan blue pencil into whose metal
neck and rubber head he's nailed
freedom's Handiwipe, red and red and white.
He wears a coat of mail, knight of the beer tops.
Steeler of the Seventies has become
warrior of the cable TV,
strategist of the constant signal.
O, bloodless glory of satellites
and star wars, reigning the sky:
"Where's my clicker?"
Like Huck, he just likes to fish,
George Washington Bush, father of the new world
order, a modern Christopher Colombia—
llore por mi, quien tiene caridad, verdad, y justicia—
slayer of dragons and natives, dark Moors, Satan.
Thanks to the Education President the Young Beast
is learning mathematics and French.
100 U.S. to 100,000+ Iraqui dead,
bless the Patriot *et les sorties*.
Bless the oily head of Schwartzkopf

that made the young one chuckle:
That's just bovine scatology.
All his heart flutters with pride
to remember Baghdad at night,
blue-green in his cube and brightening.
America's in love with himself again.
O, the hum and cruise of destruction. . . .

If he had a golden tuba he would blow it:
"Even Argentina sent a boat.
Bless the United Nations.
Free again is the emirate of Kuwait!"

13 Ways of Looking Backward

Pero a mí lo que me jalaba desde chico eran las letras, la literatura. Oiga usted—desde chamaquito—mire usted—me aventaba yo unos platotes de sopa de letra porque para mí mi ilusión verdad así era escribir novelas, como Beethoven.

Cantinflas

I

I don't know which I like better
the innocence of my not knowing something
or the embarrassment of others
for me
or not knowing

II

All poets
are L*A*N*G*U*A*G*E
poets
like an ear the size of Utah
in which there are
many fleas laughing Ha Ha

III

I make a tongue sandwich
out of peppered language.

IIII

13 x's sat quietly on a telephone wire
x   x   x   x   x   x   x   x   x   x   x   x   x
then the middle x (number 7x)
tired of the rest
turned sideways and invisible
O like Jackson it
loosed a perfect swirl of cream song
down the spiral galaxy

IIIII

I don't get it

IIIIII

Per?spec*tive to a T:
In Tuscany
Mr Walrus even sunk his tusk in me
or the panels of sight
that a fly has or
the deep blue periphery of fishood and Wittgenstein

IIIIIII

Or I still don't get it

IIIIIIII

My innocence blooms like genius:
        bluets

IIIIIIII

No, to me this is nonsense

IIIIIIIII

Nuance

IIIIIIIIII

No: nonsense

IIIIIIIIIII

Pantyhose

IIIIIIIIIIII

Maybe think about bowling
Join a bowling league

IIIIIIIIIIIII

It was evening till
Flag Day
All the duckpins flew away
We had coupons for the fish fry
where the vegetable was P's
but the alphabet soup was cold
and it was Flag Fry and Fish Day all afternoon

IIIIIIIIIIIIII

Once he drove with a woman
from Pittsburgh to Milwaukee
O, the whole milky way he drove
the only way he knew
in reverse

Pietà with a Cameo
by the Young Beast

There must be some easier way for me to get my wings.
                                    Clarence the Angel

Thirty years old with Kona-brown hair
my future's read all of the poems of W. S. Merwin
(who's still alive). She's been to Paris and Canterbury,
to Guanajuato and seen the well-preserved *momias,*
but never anything like this combination midnight swim,
coffee klatsch and martyrdom in Indiana, Pennsylvania.
A young Jimmy Stewart sits on the living room couch
dripping wet and hands her a cordial of blue
liquid. Says it's derived from flowertops. Blue roses,
perhaps. She lays her drink on a table of polished obsidian.
She asks about me. I lie in a disk arranged by track
lighting, naked, half-conscious, in white plush.
The ladies from the Welcome Wagon take their turns kicking me
in the forehead or ear. Some use spikes or serve rotini.
Young Jimmy recites his poem of a wonderful life. No—
she is insistent: she wants to know who I am,
this man who lies at the center of the world, coiled,
bloody, twitching away the last spirit of animal.
Young Jimmy offers her a ride in his Chevy Nova. Instead,
she comes to me in my death dream. To hold me in her lap.
And one by one to remove the violet petals from my brow.

One by One

With earphones
the Young Beast is listening to Mozart
on the 61C into Oakland
when the bus stops
beside a tree that is flowering

For once in his life he is not thinking
happy to be lost in all that green music

And to watch
by the Goodwill
the retarded people get on
one by one
show their transfers
like petals
and with red and yellow lunchboxes
move slowly down the aisle
their faces large
andantino
and smiling

Identity

I
in a den of me
the bear
waking like spring from the elemental dream of time

I
the bear listening
chamber music
the bright syllables of distant birds

Eye
on the wallscratching I made of myself

I
spectacled bear of the Hillman Library
devouring fillets of microfiche
carrying the body of Nietzsche on my back
a purple microdot like a wafer on my tongue
blessing the tomes and the yellow birds
davening in the Spoken Arts Department
earphoned *omphalos* to the past
a million voices rushing in the dark

I
halfunderstanding bear
falling into ravines of love
saying *I do*
walking through the burning leaves of October

I
bear of paranoia
who fear the telephone company more than hunters

the black days are back
(the Bell will snip my line like coiled brainstem
and then Delmore   whom will I talk to?)

I
vain furgod of the mirrors
combing my hair for the prowl
touching my beautiful lips
calling the baroness up for secret drinks

I
sun bear of the ordinary
lying in a field of poppies and dreaming
lying in an orange field and dreaming

I
polar bear trudging drunk and poor to the law clinic
filing for divorce
amortizing the debt of her
hating the lawyer
hating the picture of his family
hating the brown chair in which I sat

I
Asiatic
cornflower petal
hungry lonely bear

Yo
oso de nada

I
something bear
song bear
putting the needle down

once more to the point
where Mozart heard for the first time
piccolos

I
cub at my mother's nipple
sucking
sucking
sucking
a hiccup
O little lifebear

I
waking bear of scat and flowers
walking into new light
tasting the blue sky
the scent of shebear
the perfume of ammonia
I love in the seeded woods

Tepteptep

Tepteptep
being spring
his brain like
volcano
night star rain
everywhere
as always
such a brain
for thirteen

Tepteptep
sitting there
by roadside
and thinking
*why this smell
of brown hair
where there is
nobody?*
down that well
full falling
his good sense
like a book

Tepteptep
slow mumbles
*nine, ten toes
southeast wind
eaten moon
soon the bell
universe
tapestry*

ah yes yes
but but but
why this smell?

Then here come
Blackbird drunk
berry fine
flying high
earth weaving
tree crashing
falling and
laughing bird:
dingdong boy
dingdong bird
everywhere
schoolgirl hair

The Explanation

1

When I woke her
soft breath
became my wrist,
my fingers.

2

The sun.

The sun through moving leaves.

The sound of children in the street.

3

She says
the first joy is the redwing
blackbird twisting
in her pattern of flight.
And who would number the others?

4

Pray to nothing
but the light and all things,
the tiresome litter of fresh blossoms,
the whiteness of any seed.

5

Listen—
the silver throat of the carillon:
ten o'clock. My love I've wintered
long and long. Now love,
I'm calling just to call.

Absence

Here I am,
holding the receiver,
talking to no one,
my voice forever falling through these holes,
making a print for her
    to play again and again

breath on a window

Good Friday

Doomed as any bell, she lifts you in her arms again. You are flying over a small town in America. Black roofs like open matchbook covers, people tiny as toys: one mails a letter, one bends over her laundry basket, and unseen, one cries and cries in his bed. Like wildflowers, there is a sprinkling of children on a green hillside. High, faraway laughter. And there lies the cemetery, gravestones like crooked teeth. Look: a farmer rides down Main Street on a yellow tractor. A woman on the sidewalk waves to him. He waves back. The wind is peaceful that carries the gulls. Brown fields are everywhere waiting for seed. The town is happy to be alive.

She is your bride, this woman holding you in her arms. You hear her breathing. And the soft beating of her heart. Finally she lowers you to earth, at the crossing of two side streets, whispering: "Christ could be anyone. Anything." Then she hands you an orange, and it burns bright in your palm like the sun.

The Buddy Holly Poem

It's so easy
when you realize
that all the squirrels
on the shingled rooftops
of Milwaukee
are Buddha
that all trees shake green
in the wind
that the moon is you

Sing
that the whole of every note
is individual and one
that love is free
everyday
on the blue earth

Listen to me

Niño

Cuando era un cadáver,
no tenía nada,
no tenía visión,
no tenía sed,
vivía en la mitad de la nada,
dormía en una cama
de dientes de león.

Un día desnudo
me desperté en un cuarto
de muros azules,
y por primera vez
yo ví.
Me dije:
Ciego, mira.
El único,
el único que importa
          está aquí. . . .
Si tienes una voz,
úsala.
Si tienes una campana
          en tu sangre,
retúmbala.
¡Canta!

Canté
y vinieron al azul
          mil pájaros,
cada uno amarillo,
cada uno volando como un niño.

Child

When I was a corpse,
I had nothing,
no vision,
no thirst,
I lived surrounded by nothing,
I slept in a bed of dandelions.

One naked day
I woke in a room
where every wall was blue,
and for the first time
I saw.
I heard myself say:
Ciego, *look—*
the only one who matters
          is here. . . .
If you have a voice,
then use it;
like a bell
waiting in your veins,
let it go.
Sing!

I sang,
and into the blue
          came a thousand birds,
each one yellow,
each one flying like a child.

FOREWORD

This Morning in Costa Rica

Tonight the twenty-one flew
through a star-pricked indigo sky.
My friend, we don't always find the poem,
horse or cow. Sometimes we go days hungry
for milk or blood. Now one has failed two nights.

And she would die. And to let her die
with the other bellies near and full
would be slow genocide, a craziness the bats
fly from. This morning near a quiet *finca*
in a hollow tree she who has twice failed
is being fed. It is the gift of blood vomit.
It is the blessing of group love. Yes,
I think I would call it family.

Human friend, let this poem hang in your brain
upside down. Let it change us to fly out of ourselves.
This I would ask: let it echo.

Let it echo.

7   Bacatá   original tribal name for Bogotá
8   Violentólogo   Violentologist (now the study of violence is a formal discipline in Colombia)
10 Campesino   someone who lives in a rural area
12 Cofradía   Brotherhood (the term looks back to the brotherhoods of the Spanish Inquisition and forward to the contemporary, vigilante-type death squads of Colombia's urban areas)
    basuco   a type of smokable cocaine, similar to crack
13 muchachito   little boy
15 bestia   beast
    semilla   seed
    ¿Qué me cuentas?   What's up?
16 Abuelo   Grandpa
    millonarios   millionaires (also the name of a Colombian soccer team)
18 el joven bestia   the Young Beast
21 ¿Dónde está Papá?   Where's Dad?
    San Cristóbal   Saint Christopher
22 ¡Ay qué trabajo me cuesta/quererte como te quiero!   O, what work it is/to love you as I love you!
31 nieve   snow
    ferrocarril   railroad train
42 Esta voz muerta de mi madre   This dead voice of my mother
    El nueve de Abril   The ninth of April
44 La figlia che piange   The girl who cries
53 llore por mi, quien tiene caridad, verdad, y justicia   cry for me, whoever has charity, truth, and justice (from Columbus's diary in the Americas)
55 Pero a mí . . .   But what attracted me since I was a boy were letters, literature. See, since I was a kid, I filled up on huge bowls of alphabet soup because for me the real trick was to write novels, like Beethoven.
59 momias   mummies
62 Yo/oso de nada   I/nothing bear
75 finca   farm

77

Maurice Kilwein Guevara is an assistant professor of English at Indiana University of Pennsylvania, where he teaches courses in creative writing and U.S. Latino literature. In 1993 he received the Pennsylvania Council on the Arts Award for poetry and a Fulbright Senior Scholar Award in American Literature for Colombia.

The Contemporary Poetry Series

Edited by Paul Zimmer

The Contemporary Poetry Series

Edited by Bin Ramke